A WORSHIP ANTHOLOGY FOR
FESTIVALS & HOLY DAYS

H. J. RICHARDS

Kevin
Mayhew

First published in 1997 by
KEVIN MAYHEW LTD
Rattlesden
Bury St Edmunds
Suffolk IP30 0SZ

ISBN 1 84003 090 9
Catalogue No 1500151

0 1 2 3 4 5 6 7 8 9

Front cover: *God the Father* from the Isenheim Altarpiece
(detail from *The Virgin and Child with Angels*) by Mattias Grunewald (1455-1528).
Musée d'Unterlinden, Colmar, France/Giraudon/Bridgeman Art Library
Cover design by Graham Johnstone
Typesetting by Louise Hill
Printed and bound in Great Britain by
Caligraving Limited Thetford Norfolk

CONTENTS

Foreword

The previous anthologies in this series have suggested worship material for many of the feasts in the Christian calendar (Advent, Christmas, Epiphany, Easter, Ascension, Whitsun, Trinity). These are here supplemented with further suggestions, to form an introduction to the other holy days which form the Christian liturgical cycle – the feasts of the Saints.

The New Testament does not hesitate to give the title 'saint' to all Christians (see the opening lines of most of St Paul's epistles). By extension we could apply the word to the rest of the human race, all of whom are made in the image and likeness of the Holy One, and continue to be close to him in his unending love of them.

Yet we rightly specialise the title when we apply it to those who, like Jesus, have given outstanding and public witness to their godliness – the heroes and heroines of our human history: Mary the mother of Jesus, the Apostles and Evangelists, the Martyrs and the Confessors of the Faith. I have searched for readings and meditations about these, poems and prayers from different centuries and traditions, which could be used to celebrate the feasts and festivals of the Christian year, and am delighted once more to share this treasure trove with others.

H. J. RICHARDS

1 CHRISTIAN FESTIVALS

Advent

If only you would tear the heavens apart, and come,
shaking the mountains as you descend, and setting the forests alight,
convincing the doubters that you exist,
and making all the nations catch their breath,
as you work such wonders as have never been seen before!

No ear has ever heard, no eye has ever seen
any God but you who could do this
on behalf of those who long for him.
You are always ready to welcome
those who joyfully do what is right,
and who remember you because they obey you.

Yes, we have sinned and aroused your anger,
and acted like rebels against you.
We come into your presence like lepers,
our good deeds worth no more than bloody rags.
We have withered like autumn leaves
blown here and there by the fickle wind.
We have all failed to call on your name,
or to rouse ourselves and take you by the hand.
That is why your face has remained hidden,
and we, in our sins, abandoned like orphans.

And yet, O Lord, you remain our father,
you remain the potter, and we your clay,
all of us the work of your hands.
Restrain, O Lord, your anger,
do not remember our sins for ever.
Look on us all, we are your people . . .
Can you stay unmoved by our prayers?
Your silence is more than we can bear!

BOOK OF ISAIAH (C. 550 BC), 64:1-12
TRS. H. J. RICHARDS (B.1921)

Why do the Advent gospel readings repeatedly proclaim,
(is it a promise or a threat?) that the End is Nigh?
Could it be that we need reminding, at least once a year,
that Christ comes not once, but again and again?

What Christians believe in is not a 'second' coming,
but a constant coming of Christ into their lives.
Christ is not the goal towards which they are striving,
but the hub around which their lives revolve.
He 'comes' to establish the Kingdom of God,
not in the future but now.
The Kingdom is not something which we impotently yearn for.
Its coming is in our hands, and how near or far it is
depends on the extent to which we are helping to bring it about.

In the gospel readings Jesus warns his disciples
that to work for a Kingdom of God
on earth as it is in heaven
will make them unpopular.
Because it means denouncing the demonic standards
by which the world often unconsciously lives,
where the brotherhood and sisterhood of all men and women
does not even figure on the agenda.
Those who work to subvert that agenda
can expect to be persecuted.

There are not many places in the world
where Jesus's disciples are undergoing
the persecution spoken of in the gospels.
By and large the Church feels very much at ease
in our developed countries – respectable and respected.
Perhaps it is an indication that there is, at the moment,
no danger of the Day of the Lord arriving here.

H. J. RICHARDS (B.1921)

Come, my Way, my Truth, my Life:
Such a Way as gives us breath:
Such a Truth as ends all strife:
Such a Life as killeth death.

Come, my Light, my Feast, my Strength:
Such a Light as shows a feast:
Such a Feast as mends in length:
Such a Strength as makes his guest.

Come, my Joy, my Love, my Heart:
Such a Joy as none can move:
Such a Love as none can part:
Such a Heart as joyes in Love.

GEORGE HERBERT (1593-1633)

Christmas

The Christ-child lay on Mary's lap.
His hair was like a light.
(O weary, weary were the world,
But here is all aright.)

The Christ-child lay on Mary's breast,
His hair was like a star.
(O stern and cunning are the kings,
But here the true hearts are.)

The Christ-child lay on Mary's heart,
His hair was like a fire.
(O weary, weary is the world,
But here the world's desire.)

The Christ-child stood at Mary's knee,
His hair was like a crown.
And all the flowers looked up at Him,
And all the stars looked down.

G. K. CHESTERTON (1874-1936)
THE WILD KNIGHT

During the Christmas season, God is constantly saying to us:
'Do not be afraid. I am here. Your prayers have been answered.'
And perhaps we need this emphasis more than we realise.
Human beings have an incurable tendency to procrastinate.
We tend to write off the present situation
as if it is unsuitable or inconvenient,
and we keep looking forward to some ideal future
when things will run easily and smoothly.
It is the kind of attitude which Augustine had when he said,
'Lord, make me virtuous. But not yet.'
We are taught to look forward to a future heaven
and so we treat this present life as if it were a kind of hell,
or at best a purgatory.
We find our lives disorganised and full of makeshifts,
and imagine a fond future when all will be in the right order,
and our lives full of peace and beauty.
We complain of the difficulty of practising charity,
or humility, or hope, or obedience in the present circumstances,
and we sit waiting for the situation to get better,
when we think these virtues will come automatically.

It is an attitude to which we are particularly prone
when the Church is undergoing change,
when we are even more liable to dismiss the present as a makeshift,
and wait for the final set of changes.
Then, we think, we shall be able to settle down again.
Then, we imagine, we shall find everything geared for salvation.

We won't. The Kingdom is now. Salvation is in the present.
It is here and now that we have to settle down to what God has given us.
For some, this may be disturbing news.
But God assures us during this season that it is in fact the Good News.
What he is saying to us over these days is:
'When I had given you my Son, I had given you all I have.
Lift up your eyes and see that your redemption is now.
What else are you waiting for?'
And the only answer we can make is: 'Lord, that we may see.'

In times past God spoke to our fathers through the prophets.
In these times he has spoken to us through his Son.
The Word of God was made flesh and dwelt among us.
We have seen his glory.

H. J. RICHARDS (B. 1921)

Tonight the wind gnaws
with teeth of glass,
the jackdaw shivers
in caged branches of iron,
the stars have talons.

There is hunger in the mouth
of vole and badger,
silver agonies of breath
in the nostril of the fox,
ice on the rabbit's paw.

Tonight has no moon,
no food for the pilgrim.
The fruit tree is bare,
the rose bush a thorn,
and the ground bitter with stones.

But the mole sleeps, and the hedgehog
lies curled in a womb of leaves.
The bean and the wheatseed
hug their germs in the earth,
and the stream moves under the ice.

Tonight there is no moon –
but a new star opens
like a silver trumpet over the dead.
Tonight in a nest of ruins
the blessed babe is laid.

And the fir tree warms to a bloom of candles,
the child lights his lantern,
stares at his tinselled toy,
our hearts and hearths
smoulder with live ashes.

In the blood of our grief
the cold earth is suckled;
in our agony the womb
convulses its seed;
in the cry of anguish
the child's first breath is born.

LAURIE LEE (B. 1914)
CHRISTMAS LANDSCAPE

He did not send technical assistance
to our backward world –
Gabriel and a company of experts
with their know-how.

He did not negotiate
for the export of surplus grace
on a long-term loan.

He did not arrange to send us food,
or the cast-off garments of angels.

Instead, he came himself.
He hungered in the wilderness
and was stripped naked on the cross.

But hungering with us,
he became our bread,
and suffering for us,
he became our joy.

EDITH LOVEJOY PIERCE

Epiphany

The off'rings of the Eastern kings of old
Unto our Lord were incense, myrrh and gold;
Incense because a God; gold as a king;
and myrrh as to a dying man they bring.
Instead of incense (Blessed Lord) if we
Can send a sigh or fervent prayer to thee,
Instead of myrrh if we can but provide
Tears that from penitential eyes do slide,
And though we have no gold, if for our part
We can present thee with a broken heart,
Thou wilt accept: and say those Eastern kings
Did not present thee with more precious things.

NATHANIEL WANLEY

Baptism of Christ

The gospels tell us that Jesus began his public life by going down to the river Jordan to be baptised, along with countless other Jews, and that as he emerged the skies opened and a voice from heaven proclaimed, 'This is my beloved Son, in whom I am well pleased.'

The ceremony of baptism, in those days, consisted of ducking people in the river, as if they were being drowned, and then pulling them out like survivors from a shipwreck. Why did people do such a strange thing? Because they wanted to express their awareness that they were sinners, standing at a great distance from God, and longing to be close to God. They were acknowledging that they needed saving, and couldn't do anything to save themselves. So they committed themselves, as it were, into the hands of God, and trusted him to rescue them out of the waters of distress, and acknowledge them as his sons and daughters, his own dear children.

Do we find it odd to see Jesus in the midst of this company of sinners? The gospels don't. All four of them make the baptism of Jesus their lead story. He stands alongside the rest of sinners and says, 'I'm one of you, a long way from our Father in heaven, and needing to be saved.'

And when he had experienced the full distance he stood from God, and died the death we all have to die (the death that the living God can't die) – it was then that God finally rescued him. The waters of distress finally closed over his head in the grave. And it's from that that he was raised by God, with the greeting, '*Now* you are my beloved Son, in whom I am well pleased.' Jesus' baptism was a kind of dress rehearsal of his death and resurrection, when he finally revealed God as the Saver of the human race.

What a shame that so many people think of Jesus as someone coming to us from another world – a heavenly being who only looked like a man, but was really more like an angel, not needing to be saved at all. The gospels proclaim loudly that this is not so. Jesus is like the rest of us poor banished children of Adam and Eve. He entered our world as we do, a helpless babe crying out for love. He lived his life as we do, conscious that we stand a long way from God, in desperate need of salvation.

And that is good news. If it was only people from outer space whom God could call his Son, that would be bad news. Jesus showed that it is people like us, in a situation of need, that God saves, and cries out to us, 'Come home, son.' In Jesus we see what God is really like. Jesus' baptism stands out like an advertisement. It is an Epiphany of the God who is the lover of humankind.

H. J. RICHARDS (B. 1921)

Presentation or Candlemas

The feast we celebrate today is the last feast of Christmas;
the candles which we use are a symbol to remind ourselves
that Christ came to give us light and life.
The relation between light and life is felt most keenly
in the darkness of night, and during the dull days of winter.
Even in those parts of the world which are rich enough
to turn night into day with the flick of a switch,
darkness remains a threat and light a blessing.
When we pray for the dead we pray
that 'perpetual light might shine upon them',
that they will have life eternal in the radiance of heaven.

We may be good these days at lighting up our homes and streets,
but we have been less successful in combating
the interior darkness of sin, depression and despair.
It is that which gives enduring meaning to today's feast;
if we walk in the light of Christ all will be well with us,
however difficult the path we tread.

Simeon's prayer became the night prayer of the Church.
The *Nunc Dimittis* is among the most beautiful of all prayers;
to have had our way illuminated and depart in peace at the end of it,
is the fulfilment of a life lived in the service of God –
what more could we pray for as night falls?

MONICA LAWLOR

Easter

This joyful Eastertide,
away with sin and sorrow,
my love the Crucified
hath sprung to life this morrow.
    Had Christ that once was slain
    ne'er burst his three-day prison,
    our faith had been in vain:
    but now hath Christ arisen.

My flesh in hope shall rest,
and for a season slumber,
till trump from east to west
shall wake the dead in number.
    Had Christ that once was slain
    ne'er burst his three-day prison,
    our faith had been in vain:
    but now hath Christ arisen.

Death's flood hath lost his chill
since Jesus crossed the river;
lover of souls, from ill
my passing soul deliver.
    Had Christ that once was slain
    ne'er burst his three-day prison,
    our faith had been in vain:
    but now hath Christ arisen.

GEORGE RATCLIFFE WOODWARD (1848-1934)

The distinctive feature of Christianity is often thought to be
its proclamation of a hope of resurrection,
and that this means the emergence
of a genuine religion of redemption,
the main emphasis now being placed
on the far side of the boundary drawn by death.
But it seems to me that this is
just where the mistake and the danger lie.
Redemption would now mean redemption from cares, distress,
fears and longing, from sin and death,
in a better world beyond the grave.
But is this really the essential character
of the proclamation of Christ in the gospels and in Paul?
I am sure it is not.

The difference between the Christian hope of resurrection
and the mythological hope, is that the Christian hope
sends a man back to his life on earth in a wholly new way . . .
The Christian, unlike the devotees of redemption myths,
has no last line of escape available
from earthly tasks and difficulties into the eternal,
but like Christ himself ('My God, why hast thou forsaken me?')
he must drink the earthly cup to the dregs,
and only in his doing so
is the crucified and risen Lord with him,
and he crucified and risen with Christ.
The world must not be prematurely written off . . .
Redemption myths arise from human boundary experiences,
but Christ takes hold of a man at the centre of his life.

Dietrich Bonhoeffer (1906-1945)
Letters and Papers from Prison

Ascension

In the days of his earthly ministry,
only those could speak to Jesus
who came where he was.
If he was in Galilee,
they could not find him in Jerusalem;
if he was in Jerusalem,
they could not find him in Galilee.
But his Ascension means that he is perfectly united with God;
we are with him wherever we are present to God;
and that is everywhere and always.
Because he is 'in heaven', he is everywhere on earth;
because he is ascended, he is here now.

WILLIAM TEMPLE (1881-1944)
READINGS IN ST JOHN'S GOSPEL

The doctrine of the Ascension is the assertion of the absolute sovereignty of Jesus Christ over every part of this universe, the crowning of the cross, the manifest triumph of his way of love over every other force in the world. 'Angels and Authorities and Powers have been made subject to him.' That is to say, as a result of the Ascension, everything that has domination over the lives of men is ultimately in Christ's hands, including all the mysterious forces that appear to have our world in their grip, that drive us into wars that nobody wants, that plunge us willy-nilly into economic crises, and bring us to the brink of racial suicide. All the ideologies and -isms and economic bogies, the dark surging forces which work below the surface of our conscious lives, which possess men in crowds, and set class against class, black against white – these are the Angels, Authorities and Powers of our modern world. Whether we prefer to picture them as personal or impersonal, these are the things we all recognise as determining the course of history and enslaving the minds and bodies of men. The affirmation of the Ascension is that Christ really is in control of these things even when we are not, that there is no depth which his victory has not affected, no department of life in which his authority does not and must not run.

Everything that reduces more of this world – this sordid, material world of which God has chosen to be the God – to the sovereignty of Christ is a proclamation of the Gospel, an announcement to the world that Christ is in it and reigns over it. Anything, however pious and spiritual, that in fact leaves other forces in control of everyday life is a denial of the Gospel, an announcement to the world that Christ is absent from it. Ascension Day is the yearly reminder to the world of the sentence which has been served on it – that of the unconditional surrender of every part of it to the love and holiness and righteousness of Jesus Christ.

J. A. T. ROBINSON (1919-1983)
BUT THAT I CAN'T BELIEVE

Whitsun

Holy Spirit,
mighty wind of God,
inhabit our darkness,
brood over our abyss,
and speak to our chaos;
that we may breathe with your life,
and share your creation,
in the power of Jesus Christ.
Amen.

JANET MORLEY

It is done.
Once again the Fire has penetrated the earth.
Not with the sudden crash of thunderbolt,
riving the mountain tops –
does the Master break down doors to enter his own home?
Without earthquake, or thunderclap,
the flame has lit up the whole world from within.
All things individually and collectively
are penetrated and flooded by it,
from the inmost core of the tiniest atom
to the mighty sweep of the most universal laws of being:
so naturally has it flooded every element, every energy,
every connecting link in the unity of our cosmos,
that one might suppose the cosmos to have burst
spontaneously into flame.

PIERRE TEILHARD DE CHARDIN (1881-1955)
HYMN OF THE UNIVERSE

On the western slopes of the old walled Jerusalem there is a place which Christians have venerated for 1500 years as the Upper Room. The room is mentioned twice in the New Testament, once as the place where Jesus ate his last supper with his disciples, and then later as the place where the disciples, huddled together after the bewildering events of Good Friday and Easter, were bowled over (the text says) by the experience of finding themselves filled with the Spirit of the risen Christ, and went out preaching the marvels of God to anyone who cared to listen. It was the first Whit Sunday.

Few Christians who come to visit this place are aware that downstairs, across the courtyard where King David is said to have been buried, the Jews have put up a memorial to the millions upon millions of their fellow countrymen who were buried in mass graves after being rounded up, starved, stripped and gassed in Dachau, Belsen, Auschwitz, and the other Nazi concentration camps of the 30s and 40s.

What a shattering thought that these two places should be so close together, one on top of the other: the Christian Upper Room with its memories of the Eucharist and of Pentecost (Whitsun or White Sunday): and the Jewish Lower Room with its walls and ceiling black with the smoke of candles burning in memory of a holocaust. The Christian room with its echoes of Jesus's last meal with his disciples, and his words as he gave them the passover bread, 'This is my body'; and the corridor downstairs, where they still exhibit a jar with a piece of soap with a Nazi label proclaiming it was made from the bones of concentration camp victims – what poor Jew has to point at that jar and say, 'This is *my* body'? The room where Christians over the centuries have recalled the unforgettable words of Jesus as he went to his passion, that the way you would be able to tell followers of his was by the love they had for their brothers and the service they were willing to do them; and the adjoining room with its damning evidence of how miserably our Christian West learnt that lesson as we sent six million of our brothers to *their* passion.

We might claim that we personally were not directly responsible. But this hardly entitles us to look the other way and ask, 'Who is my brother?' 'Spirit of Jesus,' I have to say as I think of this Upper Room, 'come and breathe some warmth into the chilled hearts of your disciples, and me first of all.'

H. J. RICHARDS (B. 1921)

Trinity

The Hebrew Bible speaks neither of a Trinity,
nor of a God different from the God of the Gospels.
It speaks unswervingly of a *Father*, who alone creates,
teaches, liberates, loves and dwells with his people Israel,
whom he calls to become his Son.
The Gospels present Jesus as this true Israel,
who recognises God as his 'Father',
and shows the world what it means to be the *Son* of such a God,
most clearly in his death.
After his death, Jesus lives on in those who live as he did,
and who show themselves to be possessed
by the same *Spirit* of sonship that characterised his life.

In short, the reality to which people give the name 'God'
is an unfathomable mystery,
so far beyond human reach that, if he didn't breathe a word,
no one would ever know anything about him.
Christians acknowledge that there has never been a time
when *God* did not breathe a word: he has always made himself known.
But, they claim, that Word of God was never breathed more clearly
than in the life and death of *Jesus*.
And that Breath (or *Spirit*) is still felt in the inspiration
that Jesus is able to give, even after his death.
Christians claim to know the *Father* through the *Spirit* of *Jesus*.
That is what the word 'Trinity' is trying to express.

Trinity means that the one *God*
can best be found in the life and teaching of the man Jesus,
who was so filled with God's *Spirit*
that (like father like son) he can be called the *Son* of God.
His followers are those who feel themselves inspired by the same Spirit,
and know that when they live as he did,
and make his values their own,
they will be at one with God as he was.

H. J. RICHARDS (B. 1921)

Corpus Christi

Father, you have given us Jesus Christ
who is the true bread from heaven.
He is the manna of the new covenant
which came down from heaven
and gives life to the world.
Jesus said,
'I am the bread of life;
he who comes to me will not hunger,
and he who believes in me will never thirst.'
Father, deepen my faith in Christ
so he may fill me with eternal life
and raise me up on the last day.
Feed me with Christ's own body and blood,
for unless I eat his flesh and drink his blood
I will not have life in me . . .
Father, let me live by Christ your Son
as he lives by you;
and then the Spirit of holiness
by whom you raised Jesus from the dead
will dwell in me as in his temple,
and he will raise me from the dead at judgement day.
Father, I thank you for inviting me to eat at your table,
so enabling me to taste for myself
that the Lord is very sweet.

PETER DE ROSA (B. 1932)

Father, it is strange how often
the dearest things seem unfamiliar
the nearest things seem far away.
On Easter Day, Jesus was not recognised
when he walked with two of his disciples to Emmaus.
He spoke to them and listened to them;
and proved to them how necessary it was
for the Christ to suffer if he was to enter his glory.
He made them see that Calvary
was all of a piece with Moses and the prophets.
Inspired by his presence, the disciples pleaded with him,
'Stay with us, for night is coming on
and the day is almost spent.'
Christ incognito agreed and sat down with them at table.
He assumed the role of host:
he took the bread, said the blessing, broke it
and gave them a share of it.
It was through this everyday action that they knew him;
and immediately he vanished from their sight.
Father, once more Christ delivers himself
into his disciples' hands.
In the simple gesture of the breaking of the bread
he gives himself away;
and though we do not see him any more,
we believe he is always in our midst.
His Holy Spirit is a burning presence in our hearts;
and in our hands is broken and divided Bread.
Father, give us this food
that will sustain us on life's journey
and save us from being frightened
by the long and lonely night.

PETER DE ROSA (B. 1932)

Come, dear Heart!
The fields are white to harvest: come and see
As in a glass the timeless mystery
Of love, whereby we feed
On God, our bread indeed.
Torn by the sickles, see him share the smart
Of travailing Creation: maimed, despised,
Yet by his lovers the more dearly prized
Because for us he lays his beauty down –
Last toll paid by Perfection for our loss!
Trace on these fields his everlasting Cross,
And o'er the stricken sheaves the Immortal Victim's crown.

EVELYN UNDERHILL (1875-1941)
CORPUS CHRISTI

2 THE SAINTS: HOLINESS

Blest are you whose hands are empty:
You have room for God's abundance.
Come, inherit God's own Kingdom.

Blest are you who long for justice:
You will get your heart's desiring.
Come, inherit God's own Kingdom.

Blest are you whose ways are peaceful:
You are truly God's own children.
Come, inherit God's own Kingdom.

Blest are you when people hate you:
You will share the throne of Jesus.
Come, inherit God's own Kingdom.

MATTHEW 5:3-10
TRS. H. J. RICHARDS (B. 1921)

Blessed are the poor
   not the penniless, but those whose heart is free.
Blessed are those who mourn
   not those who whimper, but those who raise their voices.
Blessed are the meek
   not the soft, but those who are patient and tolerant.
Blessed are those who hunger and thirst for justice
   not those who whine, but those who struggle.
Blessed are the merciful
   not those who forget, but those who forgive.
Blessed are the pure in heart
   not those who act like angels, but those whose life is transparent.
Blessed are the peacemakers
   not those who shun conflict, but those who face it squarely.
Blessed are those who are persecuted for justice
   not because they suffer, but because they love.

MATTHEW 5:3-10
TRS. P. JACOB

Perhaps the reason why the standard of holiness among us is so low,
why our attainments are so poor,
our view of the truth so dim,
our belief so unreal,
our general notions so artificial and external, is this,
that we dare not trust each other with the secret of our hearts.
We have each the same secret, and we keep it to ourselves,
and we fear that as a cause of estrangement,
which really would be a bond of union.
We do not probe the wounds of our nature thoroughly;
we do not lay the foundation of our religious profession
in the ground of our inner man;
we make clean the outside of things;
we are amiable and friendly to each other in words and deeds,
but our love is not enlarged,
our bowels of affection are straightened
and we fear to let the intercourse begin at the root;
and in consequence our religion, viewed as a social system,
is hollow. The presence of Christ is not in it . . .
Persons think themselves isolated in the world;
they think no one ever felt as they feel.
They do not dare to expose their feelings,
lest they should find that no one understands them.
And thus they suffer to wither and decay
what was destined in God's purpose to adorn the Church's paradise
with beauty and sweetness . . .
They deny themselves the means they possess
of at once imparting instruction and gaining comfort.

JOHN HENRY NEWMAN (1801-1890)
PAROCHIAL AND PLAIN SERMONS: CHRISTIAN SYMPATHY

One good man, one man who does not
put on his religion once a week with his Sunday coat,
but wears it for his working dress,
and lets the thought of God grow into him,
and through and through him,
till everything he says and does becomes religious,
that man is worth a thousand sermons –
he is a living Gospel –
he is the image of God.
And men see his good works,
and admire them in spite of themselves,
and see that they are Godlike,
and that God's grace is no dream,
but that the Holy Spirit is still among men,
and that all nobleness and manliness
is his gift, his stamp, his picture:
and so they get a glimpse of God again
in his saints and heroes,
and glorify their Father who is in heaven.

CHARLES KINGSLEY (1819-1875)
LIVING RELIGION

The saints were not born as isolated phenomena,
but as kneaded and pressed into a common mould and feature:
into the communion of saints.
And the saint, as a member of the Church,
may be defined as one in whom the double operation
of knowledge and love of Jesus Christ
has shown most gloriously.
It is the saint who knows Christ most accurately:
precisely because that knowledge, a gift of grace,
has passed over instantaneously to love:
knowledge and love have been pressed by the anguish of life
into a single living ferment.
With grace enlightening their minds and wills,
humanity finds in them a new possibility . . .
Because they know human life,
they go without danger into any area of life.

In the Church the paradoxes of grace are commonplace:
the unlettered saint confounding the doctors:
the doctor upon the scaffold:
the man or woman of extraordinary social talent
finding fulfilment in contemplative obscurity:
the contemplative leading a crusade,
the child confounding the tyrant,
the old man singing a song in the fire of martyrdom,
the mystic sitting down with princes,
the prince in the hairshirt,
the hermit returning to set the kingdom aright.
In all of them a divine principle has come to flower:
an inner logic is directing things to a divine outcome:
in all of them the Church is mediating Jesus in time,
is still bringing forth, with a truly divine fecundity,
the sons and daughters who bear Christ into the world.

DAN BERRIGAN SJ
THE BRIDE

All liberators, all healers are sent by God; they liberate and heal through the power of the eternal given to them.

Who are these healers? Where are these saviours? The first answer is: They are *here*; they are *you*. Each of us has liberating and healing power over someone to whom you are a priest. We are all called to be priests to each other; and if priests, also physicians, counsellors, liberators.

There are innumerable degrees and kinds of saving grace. There are many people whom the evil one has enslaved so mightily that the saving power which may work through them has almost disappeared. On the other hand there are the great saving figures in whom large parts of mankind have experienced a lasting power of liberating and healing from generation to generation. Most of us are in between.

And then there is the one Saviour in whom Christianity sees the saving grace without limits, the decisive victory over the demonic powers, the tearing down of the wall of guilt which separates us from the eternal, the healer who brings to light a new reality in man and his world.

But if we call him the Saviour we must remember that *God* is the saviour *through* him, and that there are a host of liberators and healers, including ourselves, through whom the divine salvation works in all mankind. God does not leave the world at any place, in any time, without saviours – without healing power.

PAUL TILLICH (1886-1965)
THE ETERNAL NOW

I'm set on fire by who Zorba is
and how he reacts to life, Lord.
He lives life. He beholds the earth,
smells and feels it, and finds it good.
I suppose he's no saint. I'm not sure, Jesus,
what it means to be a saint right now.
(I don't think it means to act 'saintly'.
I'm afraid that kind of thing
is why people are bored with 'religion'.)
I mean, Zorba is human, Lord,
and he does good and bad things, human things.
But he seems to love life, bounces back from disasters,
meets other people's needs, and gets involved
in their lives and all of life that comes his way.
Isn't life, for Zorba,
something to be celebrated as being holy?

Do you yourself, Jesus, label some things in life as 'holy',
and others as 'profane'?
I don't think you do,
but so many people who call themselves Christians
seem to ignore you completely when they set up
their blue laws and censorship boards.
Zorba's dance of life
is a wonderful dialogue with you, Jesus.
Teach me to dance too,
or at least to be free with you,
and to understand how newness of life and renewal
are stronger than death.

NIKOS KAZANTZAKIS (1883-1957)
ZORBA THE GREEK

A Christian Reflection on the Last Judgement

Day of wrath! O Day of mourning!
See fulfilled the prophets' warning!
Heav'n and earth in ashes burning!

O, what fear man's bosom rendeth
When from heav'n the Judge descendeth,
on whose sentence all dependeth.

When the Judge his seat attaineth,
And each hidden deed arraigneth,
Nothing unavenged remaineth.

THOMAS OF CELANO (D. 1255)
DIES IRAE, TRS. W. J. IRONS

A Jewish Reflection on the Last Judgement

At the Last Judgement,
God will bring you into his presence one by one,
and there he will tell you
what your life was really about.
Then you will understand
the good you did and the bad.
And the good you did will be your heaven,
and the bad your hell.
And then God will forgive you.

SAYINGS OF THE CHASIDIM

A disciple asked the Master what was the first requirement for
    becoming a saint.
'You must be prepared to be ridiculed, ignored and starving
    until you are forty-five.'
'What will happen when I'm forty-five?'
'You'll have got used to it.'

ANTHONY DE MELLO SJ (1931-1987)

In a society whose ideals are power, possession and pleasure,
I pray that I may be a sign
of what it really means to love.
I will do my best to be a sign
that Christ Jesus alone is the Lord of history,
that he is present here in our midst,
and that he is capable of inspiring love
mightier than our instincts,
mightier than death itself.
My own desire is to lead a life in the following of Christ,
he who was poor and chaste and obedient to the will of his Father.
I wish to live for him alone and his saving work,
as his disciple.
I promise our Lord that I will be faithful,
in sickness and in health,
in youth and old age,
in tranquillity and persecution,
in joy and in sorrow.
I promise to do my best
to share in his incarnation among the poorest of the poor,
and to imitate his poverty and solidarity with them
in their struggle for freedom.
This is my hope and desire:
to share in his evangelising mission among human beings,
concentrating all the powers of my will and affections
on him and on all my sisters and brothers,
and living in continual quest of the Father's will:
in his word, in the Church,
in the signs of the times, and in the poor.

SILVIA ARRIOLA (MARTYRED 1981)
VOWS TAKEN BEFORE ARCHBISHOP ROMERO OF SAN SALVADOR

3   THE SAINTS: HOLY DAYS

January 25: Paul

Lead us, great teacher Paul, in wisdom's ways,
And lift our hearts with thine to heaven's high throne,
Till faith beholds the clear meridian blaze,
And, sun-like, in the soul reigns charity alone.

EGREGIE DOCTOR PAULE
ELPIS, WIFE OF BOETHIUS (480-524)
TRS. E. CASWALL (1814-1878)

Wrong question, Paul! 'Who am *I*, Lord?'
is what you should have asked.
And the answer, surely, 'Somebody
whom it is easy for us to kick against.'

There were some matters you were dead right
about. For instance, I like you
on love. But marriage – I would have thought
too many had been burned in that fire
for your contrast to hold.

Still, you are the mountain
the teaching of the carpenter of Nazareth
congealed into. The theologians
have walked round you for centuries
and none of them scaled you. Your letters remain
unanswered, but survive the recipients
of them. And we, pottering among the foothills
of their logic, find ourselves staring
across deep crevasses at conclusions at which
the living Jesus would not willingly have arrived.

R. S. THOMAS (B. 1913)
COVENANTERS

A parish needing a new incumbent advertised for applications through its Parish Council. A letter was eventually received from an applicant who set out his qualifications:

'I am regarded as a powerful preacher, and I have had some success as a writer. I am said to be a good organiser, and I have been a leader in most of the places to which I have gone. I have to admit that I have never preached in the same place for more than three years at a time, and that in some places I have had to leave because my work caused riots. The fact is, I have not got on too well with the religious leaders in many of the towns where I have preached. Some of them have attacked me, and even taken me to court. As a result I have been in jail four or five times, though not because of any real crime. My health is none too good, but I still manage to get a good deal done, though I am fifty years old. I have regularly worked at a trade to help me pay my way. If I can be of any use in your parish, I shall do my best for you.'

The letter was read out to the Parish Council. They all felt it must be some sort of a joke. How could they seriously consider an application from such a sickly, half-time, troublemaking ex jail-bird? In any case he was far too old. Who was he? The secretary looked at the bottom of the letter. 'The Apostle Paul.'

UNKNOWN

January 28: Thomas Aquinas

O thou our reminder of Christ crucified,
living bread, the life of us for whom he died,
lend this life to me then; feed and feast my mind,
there be thou the sweetness man was meant to find.

Jesu, whom I look at shrouded here below,
I beseech thee send me what I long for so,
some day to gaze on thee face to face in light
and be blest for ever with thy glory's sight.

ADORO TE DEVOTE
PRAYER OF ST THOMAS AQUINAS (1227-1274)
TRS. GERARD MANLEY HOPKINS (1884-1889)

March 17: Patrick

I bind unto myself today
the power of God to hold and lead:
his eye to watch, his might to say,
his ear to hearken to my need,
the wisdom of my God to teach,
his hand to guide, his shield to ward,
the word of God to give me speech,
his heavenly host to be my guard.

Christ be with me, Christ within me,
Christ behind me, Christ before me,
Christ beside me, Christ to win me,
Christ to comfort and restore me,
Christ beneath me, Christ above me,
Christ in quiet, Christ in danger,
Christ in hearts of all that love me,
Christ in mouth of friend and stranger.

BREASTPLATE OF ST PATRICK (5TH CENTURY)

March 19: Joseph

He who grew up
with wood around
ran with infant feet on sawdust ground
who in childhood played
with wooden toys made by a caring father
yet with youthful hand
learnt to whittle wood
shaping pieces to his own command.

What dreadful irony
decreed that wood should be
his instrument of death
and could it be
that Joseph once embraced
that traitor tree?

At the very end
did wood become his enemy or friend?
Did splinters stab his arms
when outstretched
for the nailing of his palms?
Or did familiarity
carve comfort even then
evoking honest kindly men
ladles or the mother's chair
and a working carpenter?

PEGGY POOLE

March 24: Gabriel

The angel Gabriel from heaven came,
his wings as drifted snow, his eyes as flame.
'All hail,' said he, 'thou lowly maiden Mary,
most highly favoured lady!' Gloria!

'For know, a blessed Mother thou shalt be,
all generations laud and honour thee;
thy Son shall be Emmanuel, by seers foretold,
most highly favoured lady!' Gloria!

Then gentle Mary meekly bowed her head,
'To me be as it pleaseth God,' she said;
'My soul shall laud and magnify his holy name.'
'Most highly favoured lady!' Gloria!

Of her, Emmanuel, the Christ, was born
in Bethlehem, all on a Christmas morn;
and Christian folk throughout the world will ever say:
'Most highly favoured lady!' Gloria!

ANGELUS AD VIRGINEM
ANON (14TH CENTURY)
TRS. SABINE BARING-GOULD (1834-1924)

March 25: Annunciation

Her morning of mornings was when one flew to bring
Some news that changed her cottage into a queen's
Palace; the table she worked at shone like gold,
And in the orchard it is suddenly spring,
All bird and blossom and fresh-painted green.
What was it the grand visitor foretold
Which made earth heaven for a village Mary?
He was saying something about a Saviour Prince,
But she only heard him say, 'You will bear a child',
And that was why the spring came. Angels carry
Such tidings often enough, but never since
To one who in such blissful ignorance smiled.

C. DAY LEWIS (1904-1972)
ON LEONARDO'S ANNUNCIATION

Let it be done to me according to thy word (Luke 1:38)
Few people realise the boldness of this punchline in the story. They read it already knowing the sequel to the story. They are already aware that Joseph is not going to abandon Mary, but will stand by her in spite of everything, and that all will turn out well.

Are they also aware that for an engaged girl to become pregnant by a third party, the penalty was death? For Mary to say, 'Let it be done' required extraordinary courage.

ANON

Nothing will ease the pain to come
Though now she sits in ecstasy
And lets it have its way with her.
The angel's shadow in the room
Is lightly lifted as if he
Had never terrified her there.

The furniture again returns
To its old simple state. She can
Take comfort from the things she knows
Though in her heart new loving burns,
Something she never gave to man
Or god before, and this god grows

Most like a man. She wonders how
To pray at all, what thanks to give
and whom to give them to. 'Alone
to all men's eyes I now must go,'
She thinks, 'And by myself must live
With a strange child that is my own.'

So from her ecstasy she moves
And turns to human things at last
(Announcing angels set aside).
It is a human child she loves
Though a god stirs beneath her breast
And great salvations grip her side.

Elizabeth Jennings

Lord, I am afraid to say 'yes'.
I am afraid of putting my hand in yours, for you hold on to it.
I am afraid of meeting your eyes, for you can win me.
I am afraid of your demands, for you are a jealous God . . .

Say 'yes'.
I need your 'yes' as I needed Mary's 'yes' to come to earth.
For it is I who must do your work,
I who must live in your family,
I who must be in your neighbourhood, and not you.
For it is my look that penetrates, and not yours,
my words that carry weight, and not yours.
my life that transforms, and not yours.
Give all to me, abandon all to me.
I need your 'yes' to be united with you and to come down to earth.
I need your 'yes' to continue saving the world.

O Lord, I am afraid of your demands, but who can resist you?
That your Kingdom may come and not mine,
that your will may be done and not mine,
Help me to say 'yes'.

MICHEL QUOIST (B. 1918)
PRAYERS OF LIFE

Pour forth, we beseech thee O Lord,
thy grace into our hearts,
that we to whom the incarnation of Christ thy Son
was made known by the message of an angel,
may by his passion and cross
be brought to the glory of his resurrection.

COLLECT FOR THE ANNUNCIATION

April 25: Mark the Evangelist

In the first part of (Mark's) gospel healings predominate. And if we did not know what was still to come, we might say, What sort of religion is this? It is a medicine, apparently, for securing health and sanity. But if science can do more for men than faith and miracle, science is the better medicine, and supernatural grace may retire from the field.

But we have no sooner formulated our objection than the scene changes. He who had healed the paralysed foot and restored the withered hand, he who had opened the eyes of the blind begins to say, 'If your hand is your undoing, cut it off and cast it from you. Off with the offending foot, out with the covetous eye; make sure of everlasting life, however the pursuit of it may maim or limit you in this present world.' He who had raised the dead before, now calls for martyrs. 'Take up your cross,' he says, 'and go with me to die.'

Ah, we say, this may be terrible, but this is religion; Christ is calling for heroes. It is not, after all, 'What can we get out of God?' that was only a beginning, a religion for children. Now it is, 'What can we do for God?' This is the religion of adults. Let us turn the page, and read the story of their finest hour.

We turn it, and what do we read?

Amen I say to thee, before the cock crows twice thou shalt thrice deny me.

He came and found them sleeping.

They all forsook him and fled.

Peter began to curse and to swear, I know not the man.

And they went out quickly and ran from the tomb, gripped by an ecstasy of terror, and said nothing to anyone, for they were afraid (the very last words of St Mark's authentic text).

Shall we reduce St Mark's Gospel to three lines?

God gives you everything.

Give everything to God.

You can't.

True, there is a fourth line: Christ will make you able, for he has risen from the dead. But this is almost overshadowed in St Mark's gospel by the emphasis on self-distrust. St Mark seems even more afraid that his readers will trust themselves than that they will distrust Christ's risen power.

AUSTIN FARRER
SAID OR SUNG

It is interesting that when Mark tells the story of Peter's famous profession of faith ('You are the Christ', 8:29), he interleaves it, unlike the other evangelists, with stories of the deaf being given their hearing (7:35) and the blind recovering their sight (8:22, 10:52). He even makes the comment that the blind have some difficulty in seeing – they can hardly distinguish people from trees (8:24), not unlike the disciples whom Jesus has to ask five times whether their sense of hearing and sight has totally left them (8:17-21). The result is that when Peter triumphantly announces, '*Now* I see, you really are the long-awaited Messiah' – and Jesus asks him whether he realises this means crucifixion and death, and Peter replies, 'Never!' – Jesus has to say, 'You're still completely deaf and blind, aren't you!' (8:33).

How difficult it is to grasp who Jesus really is, Mark warns us. How easily we go on and on misunderstanding what it means to be the Son of God.

Mark insists that people must not come to a conclusion about Jesus too quickly. There is a mystery about him. He is an enigma and a puzzle. In the kind of world we live in, no one can be a son of God without getting a good hiding, Jesus first and his disciples next. Jesus' passion and death are not some unfortunate accident: they are the very meaning of his life. Jesus is Son of God not in spite of his death but because of it. If he had *not* suffered and died, that would have proved he was not Son of God.

This means, says Mark, that until you get to the point in Jesus' life where he suffers and dies, you must keep quiet, because you've not really grasped who he is. You'd have your own interpretation of the title 'Son of God', thinking it means something like Teacher or Miracle Worker or King, and never dreaming the title might mean trouble. And that would be such a misunderstanding that Jesus would repudiate you as he did Peter. Nobody understands who Jesus is until he *stands under* the cross. It is not until then that you can say, with the centurion, 'Yes, this is the Son of God.'

Mark's gospel asks us whether, as disciples of Jesus, we can really see and hear what God is saying in his life. Do we really want God to open our eyes and ears, or does that scare us? Do we really want to be disciples of Jesus, knowing that it means being ready to shoulder the cross? Even his best friends can get it wrong.

H. J. RICHARDS (B. 1921)

May 4: English Martyrs

We praise thee, Lord, for all the martyred throng,
Those who by fire and sword or suffering long
Laid down their lives, but would not yield to wrong;
For those who fought to keep the faith secure,
For all whose hearts were selfless, strong and pure,
For those whose courage taught us to endure;
For fiery spirits, held and God-controlled,
For gentle natures by his power made bold,
For all whose gracious lives God's love retold;
Thanks be to thee, O Lord, for saints unknown,
Who by obedience to thy word have shown
That thou didst call and mark them for thine own.

BISHOP R. HEBER (1783-1826)

Most Dear and Loving Mother,
Seeing that by the severity of the laws, by the wickedness of our times, and by God's holy ordinance and appointment, my days in this life are cut off, of duty and conscience I am bound (being far from you in body but in spirit very near you) not only to crave your daily blessing, but also to write these few words unto you . . .

I had meant this spring to have seen you, if God had granted me my health and liberty, but now never shall I see you . . . Alas! sweet Mother, why do you weep? Why do you lament? Why do you take so heavily my honourable death . . . Perhaps you will say, I weep not so much for your death as I do for that you are hanged, drawn and quartered. My Sweet Mother, it is the favourablest, honourablest, and happiest death that ever could have chanced to me.

I die not for knavery, but for verity; I die not for treason, but for religion; I die not for any ill demeanour or offence committed, but only for my faith, for my conscience, for my priesthood, for my blessed Saviour Jesus Christ; and, to tell you truth, if I had ten thousand lives, I am bound to lose them all rather than to break my faith, to lose my soul, to offend my God.

We are not made to eat, drink, sleep, to go bravely, to feed daintily, to live in this wretched vale continually; but to serve God, to please God, to fear God, and to keep his commandments; which when we cannot be suffered to do, then rather must we choose to lose our lives than to desire our lives.

BLESSED WILLIAM HART (D. 1583)
FROM A LETTER TO HIS MOTHER

The righteous suffer in this world in a way that the unrighteous do not. The righteous suffer because of many things that for others seem simply natural and unavoidable. The righteous suffer because of unrighteousness, because of the senselessness and absurdity of events in the world. . . . The world says: That is how it is, always will be and must be. The righteous say: It ought not to be so; it is against God. This is how one recognises the righteous, by their suffering in just this way. They bring, as it were, the consciousness of God into the world; hence they suffer as God suffers in this world.

The Psalmist assures us that the Lord delivers the righteous. Of course, God's deliverance is not to be found in every experience of human suffering. But in the suffering of the righteous God's help is always there, because they are suffering with God. God is always present with them. The righteous know that God allows them to suffer so, in order that they may learn to love God for God's own sake. In suffering, the righteous find God. That is their deliverance. Find God in your suffering and you will find deliverance!

The answer of the righteous to the sufferings which the world causes them is to bless (1 Peter 3:9). That was the answer of God to the world which nailed Christ to the cross: blessing. . . . The world would have no hope if this were not so. The world lives and has its future by means of the blessing of God and of the righteous. . . . It is in this way that we respond to the world which causes us such suffering. We do not forsake it, cast it out, despise or condemn it. Instead, we recall it to God, we give it hope, we lay our hands upon it and say: God's blessing come upon you; may God renew you; be blessed dear world, for you belong to your creator and redeemer.

We have received God's blessing in our happiness and in our suffering. And those who have been blessed cannot help but pass this blessing on to others. Yes, wherever we are, we must ourselves be a blessing. The renewal of the world, which seems so impossible, becomes possible in the blessing of God.

Meditation from Tegel Prison, June 1944
Dietrich Bonhoeffer (1906-1945)

May 30: Joan of Arc

Do not think you can frighten me
by telling me that I am alone.
France is alone; and God is alone;
and what is my loneliness
before the loneliness of my country and my God?
I see now that the loneliness of God is his strength:
what would he be if he listened to your jealous little counsels?
Well, my loneliness shall by my strength too;
it is better to be alone with God;
his friendship will not fail me,
nor his counsel, nor his love.
In his strength I will dare, and dare, and dare,
until I die.

BERNARD SHAW (1856-1950)
ST JOAN

May 31: Visitation

My heart is bubbling over with joy;
with God it is good to be a woman.
From now on let all people proclaim:
it is a wonderful gift to be.
The one in whom power truly rests
has lifted us up to praise.
God's goodness shall fall like a shower
on the trusting of every age.
The disregarded have been raised up:
the pompous and powerful shall fall.
God has feasted the empty-bellied,
and the rich have discovered their void.
God has made good the word
given at the dawn of time.

LUKE 1:46-55
TRS. PHOEBE WILLETTS

Sing we a song of high revolt!
Make great the Lord, his name exalt!
Sing we the song that Mary sang,
of God at war with human wrong.

Sing we of him who deeply cares,
and still with us our burden bears.
He who with strength the proud disowns
brings down the mighty from their thrones.

By him the poor are lifted up;
he satisfies with bread and cup
the hungry folk of many lands;
the rich must go with empty hands.

He calls us to revolt and fight
with him for what is just and right,
to sing and live Magnificat
in crowded street and council flat.

FRED KAAN
MAGNIFICAT NOW

June 9: Columba

Alone with none but thee, my God,
I journey on my way;
What need I fear when thou art near,
O King of night and day?
More safe am I within thy hand
Than if a host did round me stand.

PRAYER OF ST COLUMBA (521-597)

My dearest Lord,
be thou a bright flame before me,
be thou a guiding star above me,
be thou a smooth path beneath me,
be thou a kindly shepherd behind me,
today and ever more.

PRAYER OF ST COLUMBA (521-597)

June 16: Richard of Chichester

Thanks be to thee, Lord Jesus Christ,
for all the benefits and blessings which thou hast give to me,
for all the pains and insults which thou hast borne for me.
O most merciful Friend, Brother and Redeemer:
may I know thee more clearly,
love thee more dearly,
and follow thee more nearly.

PRAYER OF ST RICHARD (C. 1200-1253)

June 24: John the Baptist

When you open St Mark's gospel, you find that John is defined
as a voice that shouts in the wilderness.
He is not even called a prophet, or a messenger of God.
He has become so identified with the message,
he has become so one with the word he has to proclaim to people,
that one can no longer see him behind the message,
hear the tune of his voice behind the thundering witness
of God's own spirit speaking through him.

Too often when *we* bring a message, people perceive us,
because we are not sufficiently identified with what we have to say.
In order to be identified, we must so read the Gospel,
make it so much ourselves, and ourselves so much the Gospel,
that when we speak from within it, in its name,
it should be simply the Gospel that speaks,
and we should be like a voice – God's voice.

ANTHONY BLOOM (B. 1914)
GOD AND MAN

51

John the Baptist was the only man in that society who impressed Jesus. Here was the voice of God warning his people of an impending disaster and calling for a change of heart in each and every individual. Jesus believed this and joined in with those who were determined to do something about it. He was baptised by John.

Jesus may not have agreed with John in every detail. . . . But the very fact of his baptism by John is conclusive proof of his acceptance of John's basic prophecy: Israel is heading for an unprecedented catastrophe. And in choosing to believe this prophecy, Jesus immediately shows himself to be in basic disagreement with all those who reject John and his baptism: the Zealots, Pharisees, Essenes, Sadducees, scribes and apocalyptic writers. . . .

In several of the texts that have come down to us, Jesus is far more explicit than John about what the impending disaster would entail – the destruction of Jerusalem by the Romans. . . . It was John the Baptist who first foresaw the disaster, although we do not know what exactly he envisaged. Jesus agreed with John, and reading the signs of the times saw quite clearly that Israel was on a collision course with Rome. Both Jesus and John, like the prophets of the Old Testament, expressed this imminent disaster in terms of a divine judgement. . . .

John's reaction to the coming catastrophe was negative. He tried to avert it, or save some at least from it. Jesus' reaction was positive. It was the moment of truth. The threat of imminent disaster was a unique opportunity for the kingdom to come. In the face of total destruction Jesus saw his opportunity for appealing for an immediate and radical change: 'Unless you change, you will all be destroyed.' If you do change, if you do come to believe, the kingdom will come instead of the catastrophe.

ALBERT NOLAN (B. 1934)
JESUS BEFORE CHRISTIANITY

Enough! I've kept quiet long enough,
and now I'm going to shout the truth.
I'm fed up with politicians, priests and multinationals!
Stop leading us down fifth-rate byways not even marked on a map!
Only a ten-lane highway is good enough for God –
straight as a die, straight to the point, no deceiving the people.
Politicians! Most of you are gangsters and corrupt.
The ordinary people despise your double dealing.
You have turned the God-created science of politics
Into a trough of swill fit only for pigs.
Where is truth? And justice? And compassion for the poor?
Priests! Prelates! Preachers of eternal truth!
Weak straws blowing around in the wind!
Luxurious living and private medical insurances
in a world where two out of three go to bed hungry!
Have you made a career out of the most sublime of vocations?
Put all the crap of your lives on a bonfire and burn it – now!
Stockbrokers, bankers, house-owners without a mortgage –
get rid of your excess and share what you have with the poor!
Your riches are like concrete blocks around your necks:
they'll be the death of you!
Armed Forces, Police, Prison Officers –
yours is a dangerous vocation!
Resist the temptation to take pleasure in violence.
Be in the front line of the genuine peace marches,
marching with the people, not against them.
Don't trade in your consciences for a quiet life and fat pensions!
Everyone, stop deceiving yourselves, and ask where you're going.
It is the height of idiocy to keep repeating, 'I'm a son of Abraham',
'I'm more Catholic than the Pope', 'I'm a socialist for ever'.
No, no, no!
If God wanted to, he could make the streets of Soho
holier than a Trappist monastery – but that's not the point.
You must change! He *loves* you! He *wants* you to change!
Get in the water. Get wet. Move upstream. Go against the current.
Be different! Be free! Be you!
Signed, John Baptist.

LUKE 3:1-18
JOSE LUIS CORTES (B. 1945)
THAT'S MY BOY
TRS. JOHN MEDCALF

June 29: Peter

Will you not let God manage his own business?
He was a carpenter, and knows his trade
better perhaps than we do, having had
some centuries of experience; nor will he,
like a bad workman, blame the tools wherewith
he builds his City of Zion here on earth.
For God founded his Church, not upon John,
the loved disciple, that lay so close to his heart
and knew his mind – not upon John, but Peter;
Peter the liar, Peter the coward, Peter
the rock, the common man. John was all gold,
and gold is rare; the work might wait while God
ransacked the corners of the earth to find
another John; but Peter is the stone
whereof the world is made.

DOROTHY SAYERS (1893-1957)
THE ZEAL OF THY HOUSE

When Jesus said, 'You will all fall away',
Peter said, 'The rest may fall away, but I will not.'
And Jesus replied:
 'Peter, this very night before cockcrow,
three times you will deny me.'
'No, Lord,' cried Peter, 'I would die with you
but I will not deny you.'
Then he who had lifted his head and boasted like a cock
nodded and slept three times in Gethsemane . . .
Soon afterwards, in the courtyard,
Peter denied his Master three times
at the taunt of a serving maid . . .
and he went out and wept bitterly.
Father, teach me, through Peter's humiliation,
to realise I am always weaker than I think.
Give me the light and strength of your Spirit
to resist temptation
to repent like Peter immediately I fall
and to know that Christ whom I repeatedly deny
is always looking at me
ready to forgive me
unto seventy times seven.

PETER DE ROSA (B.1932)

There's something magnificent about the way the Bible is so open and frank about its heroes. Most religious groups have taken good care to present a very hygienic portrait of their leaders. And if these leaders ever let them down in times of crisis, you'd hardly suspect it from the official documents. Yet Jews and Christians haven't been afraid to be more honest (at least, once upon a time!).

In both the Jewish and the Christian Bible, the religious leaders are again and again shown up in all their human weakness. Jacob the cheat and trickster. David the adulterer and murderer. Solomon the sensual weakling who couldn't hold his people together. The kings of Israel almost universally condemned for 'doing that which was evil in the sight of the Lord'. Even the people of Israel as a whole have their faults listed and their weaknesses exposed, in a way you or I wouldn't care to do for our own family.

And it's the same in the New Testament. The Apostles are invariably said to have been so stupid that they didn't understand what Jesus was saying. Thomas is so lacking in faith that he asks for Jesus' fingerprints, as it were, before he'll commit himself. And even Peter, the acknowledged leader of the Christian community, so loud in promises, and so poor in performance. In the long run, says the gospel, he didn't do any better than Judas himself. He betrayed Jesus just as deeply.

I find it encouraging that the Bible tells us stories like that. They're true to life. I can recognise myself in them. The good news is that people like that are forgiven.

Even Peter. Indeed, Peter's forgiveness is central to the gospel story. In a way, the whole gospel is based on his experience of being forgiven, in spite of his failure. And that gives me hope and encouragement. And I need to be encouraged like that. I need to be assured that God loves me, not because I'm godly, but because he is.

H. J. RICHARDS (B. 1921)

Bitter was the night,
Thought the cock would crow for ever.
Bitter was the night before the break of day.

Saw you passing by,
Told them all I didn't know you.
Bitter was the night before the break of day.

Told them all a lie,
And I told it three times over
Bitter was the night before the break of day.

What did Judas do?
Sold him for a bag of silver.
Bitter was the night before the break of day.

What did Judas do?
Hanged himself upon an alder.
Bitter was the night before the break of day.

Bitter was the night.
Thought there'd never be a morning.
Bitter was the night before the break of day.

Bitter was the night.
Thought the cock would crow for ever.
Bitter was the night before the break of day.

SYDNEY CARTER (B. 1925)

Heavenly Father,
help us, like Peter,
to trust you enough to obey you;
to follow though this will be to fail you;
to persist, that after our humiliation
we may hear you come again to bid us follow,
and our faith be then of rock that Satan cannot shift.

CONTEMPORARY PRAYERS
ED. CARYL MICKLEM (B. 1925)

July 3: Thomas the Apostle

Poor Thomas! Because of the brilliant story with which John brings his gospel to an end (20:24-29), he has become the Doubting Thomas, the eternal archetype of all disbelievers and sceptics. Even when he is finally forced to his knees he is not congratulated, but still being told off. 'You say you now believe, Thomas, because you've seen me. Alright. But you've got to understand that, fortunate as you are, those who believe without seeing me are more fortunate still.'

I've never met anyone who believes this to be so. Try it out. Ask people which they would prefer, actually to see and touch the risen Christ, or 'only' to believe? They'll all choose the first. For them seeing is believing. What on earth could John mean by saying that it is the second group, those who 'only' believe, who are the more fortunate?

He means that, in the deepest sense, only those who believe can 'see'. In the dramatic story, Thomas's seeing and touching obviously *feel* more real. But that is only because it is a dramatic story, not a video recording. In actual reality, no one can be in contact with the risen Christ until he believes that Jesus is alive. Do we imagine that Pilate, or Herod, or Caiaphas could have 'seen' him?

And why would people believe that Jesus is still alive after his death? Because they have experienced him as alive in the midst of the Christian community.

That goes for disciples of the first century as well as for those of the twenty-first. Believing is seeing.

H. J. RICHARDS (B. 1921)

July 6: Thomas More

O God,
who when the blessed martyr Thomas
had to choose between the allurements of the world
and the pains of imprisonment and death,
didst give him strength to embrace thy cross
with a cheerful and resolute spirit;
we pray thee grant that we too,
thanks to his intercession and example,
may fight manfully for faith and right,
and be found worthy to make a joyful entrance
into everlasting bliss.

ROMAN MISSAL

July 11: Benedict

O gracious and holy Father,
give us wisdom to perceive you,
intelligence to understand you,
diligence to seek you,
Patience to wait for you,
eyes to behold you,
a heart to meditate upon you,
and a life to proclaim you;
through the power of the Spirit
of Jesus Christ our Lord.

PRAYER OF ST BENEDICT (480-547)

The leader of a community should temper all things,
so that the strong may still have something to work for,
and the weak may not give up hope . . .
The saying is that monks ought not to drink wine.
But since today no monk believes this,
let us at least drink in moderation.

FROM THE RULE OF ST BENEDICT (480-547)

The story goes that, while he was journeying on horseback,
St Benedict met a peasant walking along the road.
'Alright for some!' said the peasant. 'Why don't I become a man
of prayer, and do all my travelling on a horse?'
'You think praying is easy?' asked Benedict. 'If you can say the Lord's
Prayer without any distraction, this horse is yours.'
'Done', said the surprised peasant.
Closing his eyes and folding his hands, he began to pray aloud:
'Our Father, who art in heaven, hallowed be thy name.
Thy kingdom come . . .'
Suddenly he stopped and looked up.
'Does that include the saddle as well?'

ANON

July 22: Mary Magdalene

You can swallow your wine at a gulp.
or make it last for an evening.
You can be busy with your body
and empty in your mind.

It is easier to feed a hungry man
than to satisfy your soul.
Easier to fill your days with busy nothings,
than to recognise your need.

Easy, it is easy to eke out your perfume
day by day,
and let the wind snatch the smell into nothing.
Easier still to keep the stopper in the jar
all your life.

It is easy to make people angry
by being yourself;
by smashing the jar.

Yet I have anointed my beloved,
I have touched his skin with my hair
and his soul with my soul.
I have filled a house with fragrance.

I have lived for an hour.
The fragrance lingers for ever.

ELAINE MILLER

July 31: Ignatius of Loyola

Teach us, good Lord,
to serve you as you deserve,
to give and not to count the cost,
to fight and not to heed the wounds,
to toil and not to seek for rest,
to work and not demand reward,
save that of knowing that we do your will,
through Jesus Christ our Lord.

PRAYER OF ST IGNATIUS (1491-1556)

August 6: Transfiguration

Father, I thank you for this gospel story
which illustrates so well Christ's sovereignty.
I believe, Lord, that in everything he says and does
he lights up and fulfils the law and the prophets;
and it is enough now to listen to him.
For Jesus is your Christ,
even though death and dereliction
are waiting for him in Jerusalem.
It will be dark there,
and on another hill, shaped like a skull,
two other men will be beside him.
From his unclothed body no light will radiate;
and even you, Father, will be silent,
except for the one word you will be saying to us
in the tremendous love of Jesus crucified.

PETER DE ROSA (B. 1932)

August 8: Dominic

Those who govern their passions are the masters of the world.
They must either rule them, or be ruled by them.
It is better to be the hammer than the anvil.

FROM THE RULE OF ST DOMINIC (1170-1221)

August 15: Mary

Virgin born, we bow before thee:
Blessed was the womb that bore thee;
Mary, Maid and Mother mild,
Blessed was she in her Child.
Blessed was the breast that fed thee;
Blessed was the hand that led thee;
Blessed was the parent's eye
That watched thy slumbering infancy.
Blessed she, by all creation,
Who brought forth the world's Salvation,
And blessed they – for ever blest –
Who love thee most and serve thee best.

BISHOP R. HEBER (1783-1826)

Queen of heaven, shout for joy,
The one you bore and raised as a boy
Has been raised from the dead, just as he said.
Pray with us to God our Father.

REGINA COELI, LAETARE (ORIGIN UNKNOWN)
TRS. H. J. RICHARDS (B. 1921)

First look with care
on her fair face:
what thou wilt see
will thee prepare
to see Christ's face
most gracefully
reflected there.

DANTE (1265-1321)
PARADISO 32, 85
TRS. PETER DE ROSA (B. 1932)

Sing of a girl in the ripening wheat,
flowers in her hand, the sun in her hair;
all the world will run to her feet
for the child that mother will bear.

Sing of a girl that the angels surround,
dust in her hands, and straw in her hair;
kings and their crowns will fall to the ground
before the child that mother will bear.

Sing of a girl on a hillside alone,
blood on her hand and grey in her hair;
sing of a body broken and torn,
oh, the child that mother will bear.

Sing of a girl a new man will meet,
hand in his hand, the wind in her hair;
joy will rise as golden as wheat
with the child that mother will bear.

Sing of a girl in a circle of love,
fire on her head, the light in her hair;
sing of the hearts the Spirit will move
to love the child that mother will bear.

Sing of a girl who will never grow old,
joy in her eyes, and gold in her hair;
through the ages men will be told
of the child that mother will bear.

DAMIAN LUNDY (1944-1996)

The baker-woman in her humble lodge
received the grain of wheat from God;
for nine whole months the grain she stored:
'Behold the handmaid of the Lord.'
Make us the bread, Mary, we need to be fed.

The baker-woman took the road which led
to Bethlehem, the House of Bread;
to knead the bread she laboured through the night,
and brought it forth about midnight.
Bake us the bread, Mary, we need to be fed.

She baked the bread for thirty years
by the fire of her love and the salt of her tears,
by the warmth of a heart so tender and bright,
and the bread was golden-brown and white.
Bring us the bread, Mary, we need to be fed.

After thirty years the bread was done;
it was taken to the town by her only son,
the soft white bread to be given free
to the hungry people of Galilee.
Give us the bread, Mary, we need to be fed.

For thirty coins the bread was sold,
and a thousand teeth, so cold, so cold,
tore it to pieces on a Friday noon,
when the sun turned black, and red the moon.
Break us the bread, Mary, we need to be fed.

But when she saw the bread so white,
the living bread she had made at night,
devoured as wolves might devour a sheep,
the baker-woman began to weep.
Weep for the bread, Mary, we need to be fed.

But the baker-woman's only son
appeared to his friends when three days had run,
on the road which to Emmaus led,
and they knew him in the breaking of bread.
Lift up your head, Mary, for now we are fed.

MARIE NOEL
LE CHANT DU PAIN
TRS. H. J. RICHARDS (B. 1921)

August 28: Augustine of Hippo

O thou who art the light of the minds that know thee,
the life of the souls that love thee,
and the strength of the wills that serve thee:
help us to know thee that we may truly love thee,
and so to love thee that we may fully serve thee,
whom to serve is perfect freedom. Amen.

PRAYER OF ST AUGUSTINE OF HIPPO (354-430)

If you really love, then when you love
you are really doing what you like.
When you keep quiet, do it out of love;
when you cry out, do it out of love;
when you correct someone, do it out of love;
when you forgive someone, do it out of love,
Let your life be utterly rooted in love:
from this root, nothing but good can grow.

ST AUGUSTINE (354-430)

You must forgive me if I do not treat every one of your words as Gospel. I must confess to your reverence that it is only to the canonical books of Scripture that I have learnt to give this sort of respect and honour. It is of these alone that I firmly believe the authors were completely free from error. So if I come across anything in these writings which seems to contradict the truth, I simply have to conclude either that my text is corrupt, or that it's a bad translation of the original, or that I've misunderstood it. But as for other writings, however holy or learned their authors, I do not accept what they say merely on their say-so.

And I presume, brother, that you agree with me on this. I presume you would wish to make a distinction between your writings and those of the Prophets and Apostles, whom it would be unthinkable to accuse of error.

LETTER TO JEROME, 82, 1
TRS. H. J. RICHARDS (B. 1921)

September 14: Holy Cross

My song is love unknown;
My Saviour's love to me;
Love to the loveless shown,
That they might lovely be.
O who am I,
That for my sake
My Lord should take
Frail flesh and die?

Sometimes they strew his way,
And sweet his praises sing;
Resounding all the day,
Hosannas to their king.
Then: Crucify!
Is all their breath
And for his death
They thirst and cry.

They rise and needs will have
My dear Lord made away;
A murderer they save,
The Prince of Life they slay.
Yet cheerful he
To suffering goes
That he his foes
From thence might free.

Here might I stay and sing,
No story so divine;
Never was love, dear King,
Never was grief like thine.
This is my Friend,
In whose sweet praise
I all my days
Could gladly spend.

SAMUEL CROSSMAN (1624-1683)

Look on thy God: Christ hidden in our flesh.
A bitter word, the cross, and bitter sight:
hard rind without, to hold the heart of heaven.
Yet sweet it is; for God upon that tree
did offer up his life: upon that rood
my Life hung, that my life might stand in God.
Christ, what am I to give thee for my life?
Unless take from thy hands the cup they hold,
to cleanse me with the precious draught of death.
What shall I do? My body to be burned?
Make myself vile? The debt's not paid out yet.
Whate'er I do, it is but I and thou,
and still do I come short, still must thou pay
my debts, O Christ; for debts thyself hadst none.
What love may balance thine? My Lord was found
in fashion like a slave, so that his slave
might find himself in fashion like his Lord.
Think you the bargain's hard, to have exchanged
the transient for the eternal, to have sold
earth to buy Heaven? More dearly God bought me.

Paulinus of Nola (353-431)
Verbum Crucis
Trs. Helen Waddell (1889-1965)

A dome superb as heaven's vault, capping a story
Whose hero blessed the meek; a desert of floor
Refracting faith like a mirage; the orchestration
Of gold and marble engulfing the still, small voice:
You cannot pass over St Peter's and what it stands for,
Whether you see it as God's vicarious throne
Or the biggest bubble yet unpricked . . .
I was lost, ill at ease here, until by chance
In a side chapel we found a woman mourning
Her son: all the *lacrimae rerum* flowed
To her gesture of grief, all life's blood from his stone.
There is no gap or discord between the divine
And the human in that pieta of Michelangelo.

C. DAY LEWIS (1904-1972)
AN ITALIAN VISIT

He who hung the earth in the void
Hangs on a gibbet for all to see;
He who fixed the heavens in their place
Has been fixed and nailed to a tree.

Has there ever been such an outrage?
Has there ever been such a sin?
The King of the heavens violated
And crucified, stripped to the skin.

Even the sun turned away from the sight,
And day was turned into night.

MELITO OF SARDIS (2ND CENTURY)
HOMILY ON THE PASSION 96
TRS. H. J. RICHARDS (B. 1921)

Who is this who comes to us in triumph,
Clothed in royal garments dyed with blood,
Walking in the greatness of his glory,
Bearing in his hand the holy rood?

This is Christ the risen Lord, the Strong one,
He who trod the wine-press all alone;
Out of death he comes with life unending,
Seeking those he purchased for his own.

Great and wonderful is our Redeemer,
Christ the living one, the just and true,
Praise him with the Father and the Spirit,
Ever with us, making all things new.

ISAIAH 63:1-7
TRS. WILLIAM HERBERT

September 21: Matthew the Evangelist

The Blessed One passed before my house,
The house that belongs to a sinner;
I ran, he turned, he waited for me,
He waited for me, a sinner.
I said, 'O may I speak to you, my Lord?'
He said, 'Yes' to me, a sinner.
I said, 'O may I follow you, my Lord?'
He said, 'Yes' to me, a sinner.
I said, 'O may I stay with you, my Lord?'
And he said, 'Yes' to me, a sinner!

BUDDHIST POEM ADAPTED FOR MATTHEW 9:9
TRS. H. J. RICHARDS (B. 1921)

September 29: St Michael and All Angels

Dear St Michael,
Heaven's glorious Commissioner of Police,
who once so neatly and successfully
cleared God's premises of all its undesirables,
look with kindly and professional eye
on our earthly Police Force.
Give us cool heads, stout hearts, hard punches,
an uncanny flair and an honest judgement.
Make us the terror of burglars,
the friends of children and law-abiding citizens,
kind to strangers, polite to bores,
strict with lawbreakers and impervious to bribery.
In trouble and riots
give us sheer muscle without temper;
at the police court
give us love for truth and evidence,
without any thought of promotion.
You know, dear St Michael,
from your experience with the Devil,
that the policeman's lot, whether in heaven or on earth,
is not always a happy one;
but your sense of duty which so surprised God,
your hard knocks which so surprised the Devil,
and your angelic self-control which so surprised both,
should be our inspiration.
Only make us as loyal to the law of God
as we are particular about the laws of the land.
And when we lay down our batons,
enrol us into your Heavenly Force,
when we shall be as proud to guard the throne of God
as we have been to guard the city.
Amen.

POLICEMAN'S PRAYER
FROM PROFESSIONAL PRAYERS BY REV A. GILLE

Angels were 'born' out of the human need to speak of God
in human language, the language of poetry and symbolism,
a language which is able to visualise the invisible,
to exteriorise the inner voice,
to personify the mystery that lies at the heart of all things.
In essence, therefore, angels are a language about God, not themselves.
The most prominent name in the mythology of angels emphasises this:
the word Michael means literally 'Who is like God?',
in other words, 'Nothing takes the place of God, not even me.'

Of God, the language of angels says this:
that he is a reality to be adored and praised;
that he transcends all that is human with a majesty
beyond that of all earthly kings and rulers;
that he is nonetheless present among us, not distant from us,
knowing us and revealing himself to us, not hiding from us;
that his power and activity are exercised here on earth not in heaven;
that his power is to protect and support
and lead the human race to union with himself.
The task of an angel is not to keep God at a safe distance
but to bring him into the world.

To read something about angels
is to read something about God.
Angels never speak about themselves, only about God.
We do not know what angels are, only what they mean,
namely, the majesty and transcendence,
the protection and the revelation of God.
Stories about angels ensure that this truth
can not only be expressed but preserved
as they are handed on from one generation to the next.

H. J. RICHARDS (B. 1921)
THE FIRST CHRISTMAS: WHAT REALLY HAPPENED?

October 4: Francis of Assisi

Lord, make me an instrument of your peace.
Where there is hatred, let me sow love;
where there is injury, pardon;
where there is discord, unity;
where there is doubt, faith;
where there is despair, hope;
where there is darkness, light;
where there is sadness, joy.

PRAYER OF ST FRANCIS (1181-1226)

In the looking glass of Francis
It's a young man that I see
And he's piping for the dancers
In the fields of Galilee.

Did you dance, and did you revel
Till the night became the day
Like the young man of Assisi?
Mark and Matthew never say.

In the looking glass of Francis
It's a young man that I see
And the Romans go a-riding
Through the fields of Galilee.

Were you always meek and gentle?
Francis longed to be a knight.
Did you never wonder whether
You should take the sword to fight?

In the looking glass of Francis
It's a young man that I see
And the lovers go a-laughing
Through the fields of Galilee.

Did you never love a woman
Like the young men of today
With your soul and with your body?
Mark and Matthew never say.

Mark and Matthew never tell me,
Luke and John are silent too
When I ask them for the story
Of the young man that was you.

In the looking glass of Francis
It's the young man that I see
And he's piping for the dancers
In the fields of Galilee.

SYDNEY CARTER (B. 1925)

Laudato sii, o mi Signore
May you be praised, my Lord.

Yes, be praised in all your creatures,
Brother Sun and Sister Moon,
In the stars and in the wind,
Air and fire and flowing water.

For our sister, Mother Earth,
She who feeds us and sustains us,
For her fruits, her grass, her flowers,
For the mountains and the oceans.

Praise for those who spread forgiveness,
Those who share your peace with others,
Bearing trials and sickness bravely:
Even Sister Death won't harm them.

Praise to you, Father most holy,
Praise and thanks to you, Lord Jesus,
Praise to you, most holy Spirit,
Life and joy of all creation.

Laudato sii, o mi Signore
May you be praised, my Lord.

FRANCIS OF ASSISI (1181-1226)
TRS. DAMIAN LUNDY (1944-1996)

October 15: Teresa of Avila

Let nothing disturb you, nothing alarm you:
while all things fade away
God is unchanging.
Be patient
and you will gain everything:
for with God in your heart
nothing is lacking,
God meets your every need.

Govern all by your wisdom, O Lord,
so that my soul may always be serving you as you will,
and not as I choose.
Do not punish me, I implore you,
by granting that which I wish or ask,
if it offend your love,
which would always live in me.
Let me die to myself, that so I may serve you;
let me live to you who in yourself are the true life.
Amen.

St Teresa of Avila (1515-1582)

October 17: Ignatius of Antioch

The wild beasts will soon provide my way to God.
I am God's wheat, ready to be ground fine by lions' teeth
to become the purest bread for Christ.
Better still if the beasts leave no scrap of my flesh,
so that I need not be a burden to anyone after I fall asleep.
When there is no trace of my body left for the world to see,
then I shall truly be Jesus Christ's disciple . . .
Earthly longings have been crucified,
leaving only a murmur of living water that whispers within me,
'Come to the Father.'

LETTER TO THE ROMANS, 4-7
ST IGNATIUS OF ANTIOCH (D. 107)

October 18: St Luke

Dear St Luke,
doctor and medical adviser to St Paul,
guide my hand and my eye
for the sake of my patient.
Steady my nerves and my scalpel;
make muscles, veins, arteries and nerves
behave according to the book;
and keep an eye on the anaesthetist.
Save us all from lapses of memory,
fraying of tempers,
confusion of bottles and instruments,
miscounting of swabs and blunders of diagnosis.
If it is 'kill or cure', please cure,
If it is 'kill or maim', please maim,
but save my patient and my reputation.

SURGEON'S PRAYER
FROM PROFESSIONAL PRAYERS BY REV A. GILLE

November 1: All Saints

How mighty are the Sabbaths,
how mighty and how deep,
that the high courts of heaven
to everlasting keep.
What peace unto the weary,
what pride unto the strong,
when God to whom are all things
shall be all things to men.

But of the courts of heaven
and him who is the King,
the rest and the refreshing,
the joy that is therein,
let those that know it answer
who in that bliss have part,
if any word can utter
the fullness of the heart.

There Sabbath unto Sabbath
succeeds eternally,
the joy that has no ending
of souls in holiday.
And never shall the rapture
beyond all mortal ken
cease from the eternal chorus
that angels sing with men.

PETER ABELARD (1079-1142)
O QUANTA QUALIA
TRS. HELEN WADDELL (1889-1965)

We thank you, Lord, for those who knew that they were poor;
may the Kingdom of Heaven be always theirs:
John the Baptist, forerunner, prophet, yet much more than a prophet;
Francis of Assisi, brother to every creature under the sun;
Ignatius Loyola, prince of paupers, missionary extraordinaire;
John Bunyan, tinker, poet, prisoner for the Lord's sake.

We thank you, Lord, for those who mourned
while waiting for your Kingdom;
may they find consolation:
Jeremiah, lamenting, suffering prophet of the exile;
Mary of Magdala, whose tears prepared your corpse for a new life;
Dante Alighieri, whose ray of hope transcends the flame of Hell;
William Blake, visionary, artist longing to possess the infinite.

We thank you, Lord, for those of a gentle spirit;
may the earth be their possession:
Peter Abelard and Eloise, lovers of life, lovers of God;
Albert Schweitzer, of masterful mind yet serving spirit;
Simone Weil, waiting on God by waiting on men;
Good Pope John XXIII, humble champion of reform.

We thank you, Lord, for those who hungered and thirsted
for what is right;
may they be satisfied:
Patrick, binding to Christ a nation disunited;
Thomas More, man of conscience, man for all seasons;
John Wesley, disturbing the peace of the complacent;
William Booth, General of God's Army.

We thank you, Lord, for those who showed mercy;
may mercy always be shown to them:
David, psalmist, who blessed your enemies;
Stephen, martyr, who forgave his executors;
Florence Nightingale, whose light shone in dark places.

We thank you, Lord, for those whose hearts were pure;
may they ever look on God:
George Fox, pulling down the pillars of the world;
John Newman, cardinal of great virtue;
William Temple, archbishop, workman for God.

We thank you, Lord, for peacemakers;
may they be called children of God:
Abraham Lincoln, dedicated liberator of the enslaved;

Mahatma Gandhi, undaunted apostle of non-violence;
Dag Hammarskjöld, untiring servant of the nations;
Abbé Paul Couturier, inspired father of unity.

We thank you, Lord, for those who suffered persecution
for the cause of right:
may the Kingdom of Heaven be always theirs:
Peter, Paul, apostles, saints, victorious martyrs;
Thomas of Canterbury, tradesman's son, chancellor, archbishop;
Joan of Arc, Maid of Orleans, inspiration of armies;
Dietrich Bonhoeffer, philosopher, protester, prisoner.

With all these witnesses to faith around us like a cloud,
we pledge ourselves, with God's help,
to throw off every encumbrance, every sin to which we cling,
and run with resolution the race we have started.
We will never lose sight of Jesus,
on whom our faith depends from start to finish;
may he lead us on to share the perfection of his saints. Amen.

BRIAN FROST AND DEREK WENSLEY

We thank you, God, for the saints of all ages;
for those who in times of darkness
kept the lamp of faith burning;
for the great souls who saw visions of larger truth
and dared to declare it;
for the multitude of quiet and gracious souls
whose presence has purified and sanctified the world;
and for those known and loved by us
who have passed from this earthly fellowship
into the fuller light of life with you.

ANON

Not throned above the skies,
Nor golden-walled afar,
But where Christ's two or three
In his name gathered are,
Be in the midst of them,
God's own Jerusalem.

F. T. PALGRAVE (1824-1897)
O THOU NOT MADE

November 2: The Faithful Departed

Abide with me, fast falls the eventide;
The darkness deepens; Lord, with me abide;
When other helpers fail, and comforts flee,
Help of the helpless, O abide with me.

Swift to its close ebbs out life's little day;
Earth's joys grow dim, its glories pass away;
Change and decay in all around I see;
O thou that changest not, abide with me.

I fear no foe with thee at hand to bless;
Ills have no weight and tears no bitterness.
Where is death's sting? Where, grave, thy victory?
I triumph still if thou abide with me.

HENRY FRANCIS LYTE (1793-1847)

God be in my head, and in my understanding;
God be in my eyes, and in my looking;
God be in my mouth, and in my speaking;
God be in my heart, and in my thinking;
God be at my end, and at my departing.

BOOK OF HOURS (1514)

O strength and stay upholding all creation,
Who ever dost thyself unmoved abide,
Yet day by day the light in due gradation
From hour to hour through all its changes guide,
Grant to life's day a calm unclouded ending,
An eve untouched by shadows of decay,
The brightness of a holy death-bed blending
With dawning glories of the eternal day.

PRAYER OF ST AMBROSE OF MILAN (339-397)
RERUM DEUS TENAX VIGOR
TRS. J. ELLERTON AND F. HART

My friends, we will not go again or ape an ancient rage,
Or stretch the folly of our youth to be the shame of age,
But walk with clearer eyes and ears this path that wandereth,
And see undrugged in evening light the decent inn of death;
For there is good news yet to hear and fine things to be seen,
Before we go to Paradise by way of Kensal Green.

G. K. CHESTERTON (1874-1936)
THE ROLLING ENGLISH ROAD

December 7: Ambrose

Now with the fast departing light,
Maker of all, we ask of thee,
Of thy great mercy, through the night
Our guardian and defence to be.
Far off let idle visions fly,
No phantom of the night molest,
Curb thou our raging enemy,
That we in chaste repose may rest.

PRAYER OF ST AMBROSE OF MILAN (339-397)
TE LUCIS ANTE TERMINUM
TRS. E. CASWALL (1814-1878)

December 26: Stephen

Grant, O Lord,
that in all our sufferings here upon earth
for the testimony of thy truth,
we may steadfastly look up to heaven,
and by faith behold the glory that shall be revealed;
and being filled with the holy Spirit,
may learn to love and bless our persecutors
by the example of thy first Martyr Saint Stephen,
who prayed for his murderers to thee, O blessed Jesus,
who standest at the right hand of God
to succour all those that suffer for thee,
our only Mediator and Advocate.
Amen.

COLLECT FOR ST STEPHEN'S DAY
BOOK OF COMMON PRAYER

December 27: John the Evangelist

I never thought to call down fire on such,
Or, as in wonderful and early days,
Pick up the scorpion, tread the serpent dumb;
But patient stated much of the Lord's life
Forgotten or misdelivered, and let it work:
Since much that at the first, in deed and word,
Lay simply and sufficiently exposed,
Had grown . . .
Of new significance and fresh result;
What first were guessed as points, I now knew stars,
And named them in the Gospel I have writ . . .
To me, that story – ay, that Life and Death
Of which I wrote 'it was' – to me, it is;
– Is, here and now: I apprehend nought else.

ROBERT BROWNING (1812-1889)
A DEATH IN A DESERT

It was there from the beginning,
but it's now been spoken to us,
and we've heard it with our own ears,
and we've touched it with our hands:
    The Word, the Word of Life,
    The lifegiving Word, the Word about God.

We have seen it with our own eyes;
we want you to see it also;
it's the life which God is living,
and it's shone into our lives.
We have seen it, we have heard it,
and we want to share it with you:
it's the life we share with God
and with his own Son, Jesus Christ.
And we're writing this to tell you –
we want you to hear the good news,
we want you to share it with us,
so that our joy can be yours:
    The Word, the Word of Life,
    The lifegiving Word, the Word about God.

FIRST EPISTLE OF JOHN 1:1-4
TRS. H. J. RICHARDS (B. 1921)

December 28: Holy Innocents

Listen to the wailing in Judea,
the cry of bitter lamentation!
It is Israel sobbing for her children,
and refusing to be comforted,
because not one is left.

But the Lord has this to say:
'Stop your tears and dry your eyes.
Amends will be made for your suffering;
there is hope for your future still:
your children will come back home . . .

The children of Israel remain my children,
dear to me and close to my heart.
Whatever their misfortune, I remember them,
and my heart is moved with compassion.
This is the word of the Lord.'

BOOK OF JEREMIAH 31:15-20
TRS. H. J. RICHARDS (B. 1921)

December 29: Thomas of Canterbury

We thank Thee for Thy mercies of blood,
   for Thy redemption by blood.
For the blood of Thy martyrs and saints
Shall enrich the earth, shall create the holy places.

For wherever a saint has dwelt,
   wherever a martyr has given his blood for the blood of Christ,
There is holy ground, and the sanctity shall not depart from it
Though armies trample over it,
   though sightseers come with guide-books looking over it;

From where the western seas gnaw at the coast of Iona,
To the death in the desert,
   the prayer in forgotten places by the broken imperial column,
From such ground springs that which forever renews the earth
Though it is forever denied. Therefore, O God, we thank Thee
Who hast given such blessing to Canterbury.

T. S. ELIOT (1888-1965)
MURDER IN THE CATHEDRAL

4 BIDDING PRAYERS

Lord God,
the story of your love for us makes us realise
that there are many others as well as ourselves
who need your help and your grace.
So we bring our prayers to you:

For those who suffer pain,
Lord, in your mercy, hear our prayer.

For those whose minds are disturbed,
or have never matured,
Lord, in your mercy, hear our prayer.

For those who have not had the opportunity
to realise their potentialities,
Lord, in your mercy, hear our prayer.

For those who are satisfied with something less
than the life for which they were made,
Lord, in your mercy, hear our prayer.

For those who know their guilt, their shallowness, their need,
but do not know the good news brought by Jesus,
Lord, in your mercy, hear our prayer.

For those who know that they must shortly die,
Lord, in your mercy, hear our prayer.

For those who cannot wait to die,
Lord, in your mercy, hear our prayer.

Help us, who offer these prayers,
to take the sufferings of others upon ourselves,
and so, by your grace,
become the agents of your transforming love.

CONTEMPORARY PRAYERS
ED. CARYL MICKLEM (B. 1925)

Jesus, preaching the good news to the poor,
proclaiming release to the captives,
setting free those who are in chains,
    we commit ourselves to you.

Jesus, friend of the poor,
feeder of the hungry,
healer of the sick,
    we commit ourselves to you.

Jesus, denouncing the oppressor,
instructing the simple,
going about doing good,
    we commit ourselves to you.

Jesus, teacher of patience,
pattern of gentleness,
prophet of the Kingdom of God,
    we commit ourselves to you.

5   A Selection of Collects

1   O Almighty God,
who hast knit together thine elect
in one communion and fellowship,
in the mystical body of thy Son Christ our Lord;
grant us grace so to follow thy blessed Saints
in all virtuous and godly living,
that we may come to those unspeakable joys,
which thou hast prepared
for them that unfeignedly love thee;
through Jesus Christ our Lord. Amen.

COLLECT FOR ALL SAINTS' DAY
BOOK OF COMMON PRAYER

2   O God of love,
who hast given us a new commandment
through thine only-begotten Son,
that we should love one another,
even as thou didst love us,
the unworthy and the wandering,
and gavest thy beloved Son
for our life and salvation:
we pray thee give us, thy servants,
in all the time of our life on earth,
a mind forgetful of past ill-will,
a pure conscience, sincere thoughts,
and a heart to love our brethren:
for the sake of Jesus Christ thy Son,
our Lord and Saviour. Amen.

FROM THE COPTIC LITURGY OF ST CYRIL

3   Grant, O God,
that the ears that have heard the voice of thy songs
may be closed to the voice of clamour and dispute;
that the eyes that have seen thy great love
may also behold thy blessed hope;
that the tongues which have sung thy praise
may speak the truth;
that the feet which have walked thy courts
may walk in the region of light;
that the bodies which have partaken of thy living Body
may be restored to newness of life.
Glory be to thee for thine unspeakable gift.

FROM THE MALABAR LITURGY (5TH CENTURY)

4   Though our mouths were full of song as the sea,
and our tongues of exultation as the multitude of its waves,
and our lips of praise as the wide-extended firmament;
though our eyes shone with the light like the sun and the moon,
and our hands were spread forth like the eagles of heaven,
we should still be unable to thank thee and to bless thy name,
O Lord our God and God of our fathers,
for one thousandth or one ten-thousandth part
of the bounties which thou hast bestowed on our fathers and us.

JEWISH PRAYER

5   Bless us, O Lord,
through your holy feasts,
and fill us with living joy
and peace in our hearts.
Bless us now and always,
and make us holy
as we obey your holy law.
Fill us with your goodness
and gladden our souls
with your salvation.
Purify our hearts
as we serve you in love and truth
and welcome with joy and gratitude
your holy festivals.

JEWISH PRAYER FOR FESTIVALS
TALMUD, BER. 9, 3

6   Grant peace, welfare, blessing, grace,
loving kindness and mercy to all mankind, O Lord.
Bless us, even all of us together,
with the light of thy countenance,
for it is thy light in dark times
which gives us blessings and mercy,
light and peace.
Give us the strength and courage
to reach out for these blessings
and to share them with our neighbour.
Blessed art thou, O Lord,
who blessest thy people at all times
and in every hour with thy peace.

JEWISH PRAYER

7   May we rid our hearts and minds
of greed, anger and delusion,
so that we become centres of peacefulness,
reaching out to others.
May those we meet
feel the sincerity of our intentions,
so that they may also radiate
the love which alone destroys hatred.
May every blessing rest upon those
who strive for understanding
between peoples of differing faiths and cultures,
and let us respect the ideas of others
whilst preserving what is good in our own traditions.
Peace to all beings, everywhere.

BUDDHIST PRAYER

8   O God, early in the morning I cry to you.
Help me to pray
and to concentrate my thoughts on you;
I cannot do this alone.
In me there is darkness,
but with you there is light;
I am lonely, but you do not leave me;
I am feeble in heart, but with you there is help;
I am restless, but with you there is peace.
In me there is bitterness, but with you there is patience;
I do not understand your ways,
but you know the way for me.

DIETRICH BONHOEFFER (1906-1945)
MORNING PRAYER, CHRISTMAS 1943

9   Lord Jesus Christ,
Son of the living God,
Comforter of widows,
Washer of feet,
show us how to care for each other.
Teach us to love as you did –
unconditionally, unilaterally,
without fear or favour,
pride or prejudice.
Give us open hearts
and wise minds
and hands that are worthy
to serve in your name.

SHEILA CASSIDY (B. 1937)

10   O God, we praise you
for the multitudes of women, men,
young people and children,
who are seeking to be witnesses
of peace, trust, and reconciliation
throughout the world.
In the footsteps of the holy witnesses
of all the ages, from Mary and the apostles
to the believers of today,
grant us to prepare ourselves inwardly,
day after day, to place our trust
in the mystery of faith.

BROTHER ROGER OF TAIZÉ
LIFE FROM WITHIN

11   O Lord, open my eyes
        that I may see the need of others;
        open my ears that I may hear their cries;
        open my heart so that they need not be without succour.
        Let me not be afraid to defend the weak
        because of the anger of the strong,
        nor afraid to defend the poor
        because of the anger of the rich.
        Show me where love and hope and faith are needed,
        and use me to bring them to these places.
        Open my eyes and ears that I may, this coming day,
        be able to do some work of peace for thee.

        ALAN PATON (1903-1988)
        PRAYERS FOR PEACE

12   Lord Jesus Christ,
        you are the voice of the living God,
        the light and likeness of his glory.
        You did not spare your own life,
        but shed your blood and gave your soul.
        You went out to seek us,
        and you died to find us.
        We pray that,
        strengthened and inspired by you,
        we may do for each other
        what you have done for us.
        Give us the strength to be
        as good to each other as God.

        HUUB OOSTERHUIS
        YOUR WORD IS NEAR

13   Lord God,
we are not your peace in this world.
We are not your remedy and salvation
for people who are broken and divided,
because we are ourselves divided,
petty-minded and intransigent.
We betray your cause and spread confusion.
But you can give us the beginning of unity.
Make us at least see
the folly of our division.
Make us feel sorry for it
and no longer content to stay where we are.
Help us to think and act
in the light of your future,
your promise to make everything new.

HUUB OOSTERHUIS
YOUR WORD IS NEAR

14   Thanks be to thee, O Christ,
because thou hast broken for us
the bonds of sin
and brought us into fellowship
with the Father.
Thanks be to thee, O Christ,
because thou hast overcome death
and opened to us
the gates of eternal life.
Thanks be to thee, O Christ,
because where two or three are gathered together
in thy name
there art thou in the midst of them.
Thanks be to thee, O Christ,
because thou ever livest
to make intercession for us.
Amen.

ANON

CALENDAR OF HOLY DAYS

January	6	Epiphany
	7	Baptism of Christ
	25	Paul
	28	Thomas Aquinas
February	2	Presentation
March	17	Patrick
	19	Joseph
	24	Gabriel
	25	Annunciation
April	25	Mark Evangelist
May	4	English Martyrs
	30	Joan of Arc
	31	Visitation
June	9	Columba
	16	Richard of Chichester
	24	John Baptist
	29	Peter
July	3	Thomas Apostle
	6	Thomas More
	11	Benedict
	22	Mary Magdalene
	31	Ignatius Loyola
August	6	Transfiguration
	8	Dominic
	15	Mary
	28	Augustine of Hippo
September	14	Holy Cross
	21	Matthew Evangelist
	29	Michael and all Angels
October	4	Francis of Assisi
	15	Teresa of Avila
	17	Ignatius of Antioch
	18	Luke Evangelist
November	1	All Saints
	2	Faithful Departed
December	7	Ambrose
	25	Christmas
	26	Stephen
	27	John Evangelist
	28	Holy Innocents
	29	Thomas of Canterbury

Index of Authors and Translators

ACKNOWLEDGEMENTS

Except where mentioned, the Scripture readings in this anthology are translations by H. J. Richards, © copyright 1997 by Kevin Mayhew Ltd.

The publishers wish to express their gratitude to the following for permission to reproduce copyright material in this publication:

Baptist Missionary Society, PO Box 49, Baptist House, 129 Broadway, Didcot, Oxfordshire OX11 8XA, for the translation by P. Jacob of Matthew 5:3-10.

CAFOD, 2 Romero Close, Stockwell Road, London SW9 9TY for an extract from *Continent of Hope.*

Cassell plc, Wellington House, 125 Strand, London WC2R 0BB, for *Epiphany* by Nathaniel Wanley © 1972 Geoffrey Chapman (an imprint of Cassell plc); *Corpus Christi* by Evelyn Underhill © 1972 Geoffrey Chapman; the translation of *Isaiah 63:1-7* by William Herbert © 1972 Geoffrey Chapman; and the collect by Brother Roger of Taizé from *Life From Within* © 1990 Geoffrey Chapman Mowbray (an imprint of Cassell plc).

The Christian Century, 407 S. Dearborn Street, Suite 1405, Chicago, IL 60605-1150, USA, for *For Our Sake* by Edith Lovejoy Pierce.

Constable and Co. Ltd, 3 The Lanchesters, 162 Fulham Palace Road, London W6 9ER, for two extracts from *Mediaeval Latin Lyrics* translated by Helen Waddell.

Darton Longman & Todd Ltd, 1 Spencer Court, 140-142 Wandsworth High Street, London SW18 4JJ, for extracts from *Jesus Before Christianity* by Albert Nolan, published and copyright 1977; *God and Man* by Anthony Bloom published and copyright 1971; and *Good Friday People* by Sheila Cassidy published and copyright 1991; used by permission of the publishers.

Mr Peter De Rosa for his translation of *Paradiso 32, 58.*

Faber & Faber Limited, 3 Queen Square, London WC1N 3AU, for extracts from *Zorba the Greek* by Nikos Kazantzakis, and *Murder in the Cathedral* by T. S. Eliot.

Gill & Macmillan, Goldenbridge, Dublin 8, Ireland, for an extract from *Help Me to Say 'Yes'* from *Prayers of Life* by Michel Quoist.

Mr David Gracie for his translation of *Meditation from Tegel Prison* by Dietrich Bonhoeffer.

HarperCollins Publishers, 77-85 Fulham Palace Road, Hammersmith, London W6 8JB, for *Joseph* by Peggy Poole and *Mary Magdalene* by Elaine Miller from *New Christian Poetry*; *Corpus Christi* and *Transfiguration* by Peter De Rosa from *A Bible Prayer Book for Today*; *It Is Done . . .* by Pierre Teilhard de Chardin from *Hymn of the Universe; Enough, I've Kept Quiet* from *That's My Boy* translated by John Medcalf.

David Higham Associates Ltd, 508 Lower John Street, Golden Square, London W1R 4HA, for *The Annunciation* by Elizabeth Jennings from *A Sense of the World*, and for an extract from *The Zeal of Thy House* by Dorothy L. Sayers.

Macmillan Press Ltd, Houndmills, Basingstoke, Hampshire RG21 6XS, for an extract from *Readings in St John's Gospel* by William Temple.

The Alan Paton Trust, c/o Frances Bond Literary Services, PO Box 223, Westville 3630, KwaZulu, Republic of South Africa, for an extract from *Instrument of Thy Peace* by Alan Paton.

Penguin Books Ltd, Bath Road, Harmondsworth, Middlesex UB7 0DA, for an extract from *Bloom of Candles* by Laurie Lee.

SCM Press, 9-17 St Albans Place, London N1 0NX, for two extracts (adapted) from Dietrich Bonhoeffer *Letters and Papers from Prison* The Enlarged Edition, SCM Press 1971; two prayers from *Contemporary Prayers for Public Worship* edited by Caryl Micklem, SCM Press 1967; and one extract from *The Eternal Now* by Paul Tillich, SCM Press 1963.

The Society of Authors (on behalf of the Bernard Shaw Estate), 84 Drayton Gardens, London SW10 9SB, for extract from *Saint Joan* by Bernard Shaw.

SPCK, Holy Trinity Church, Marylebone Road, London NW1 4DU, for the prayer by Janet Morley from *All Desires Known*.

Stainer & Bell Ltd, PO Box 110, Victoria House, 23 Gruneisen Road, Finchley, London N3 1DZ, for *Sing We a Song* by Fred Kaan © 1968 Stainer & Bell Ltd, *Bitter Was the Night* by Sydney Carter © 1964 Stainer & Bell Ltd, *In the Looking Glass of Francis* by Sydney Carter © 1980 Stainer & Bell Ltd, and *We Thank You, Lord* by Brian Frost and Derek Wensley © 1970 Stainer & Bell Ltd.

Mr R. S. Thomas for *Covenanters*.

Twenty-Third Publications, PO Box 180, 185 Willow Street, Mystic, CT 06355, USA, for an extract from *The First Christmas: What Really Happened* by H. J. Richards.

A. P. Watt Ltd (on behalf of The Royal Literary Fund), 20 John Street, London WC1N 2DR, for *Christmas* from *The Wild Knight* by G. K. Chesterton, and an extract from *The Rolling English Road* by G. K. Chesterton.

Rev. Alfred Willetts for *Magnificat* by Phoebe Willetts.

The following are © copyright Kevin Mayhew Ltd: *Sing of a Girl* and *Laudato Sii, O Mi Signore* by Damian Lundy; an extract by Monica Lawlor from *Proclaim the Word*.

Copyright Control: extracts from *Professional Prayers* by Rev. A. Gille; the Prayer for St Thomas More; extract from *Said or Sung* by Austin Farrer; *This Joyful Eastertide* by George Ratcliffe Woodward; the Collects by Huub Oosterhuis.

Every effort has been made to trace the owners of the copyright material included in this publication and we hope that no copyright has been infringed. Pardon is sought and apology made if the contrary be the case, and a correction will be made in any reprint of this book.